www.raintreepublishers.co.uk
Visit our website to find out
more information about
Raintree books.

To order:
☎ Phone 0845 6044371
🖺 Fax +44 (0) 1865 312263
🖳 Email myorders@raintreepublishers.co.uk

Customers from outside the UK please telephone +44 1865 312262

©Raintree is an imprint of Capstone Global Library
Limited, a company incorporated in England and Wales
having its registered office at 7 Pilgrim Street, London,
EC4V 6LB – Registered company number: 6695582

Text © Capstone Global Library Limited 2010
First published in hardback in 2010
First published in paperback in 2011
The moral rights of the proprietor have been asserted.

Edited by Nancy Dickmann, Sian Smith, and
  Rebecca Rissman
Designed by Joanna Hinton Malivoire
Original illustrations ©Capstone Global Library 2010
Original illustrations by Christian Slade
Picture research by Tracy Cummins
Originated by Capstone Global Library Ltd
Printed and bound in China by Leo Paper Products Ltd

ISBN 978 1 4062 1306 5 (hardback)
14 13 12 11 10
10 9 8 7 6 5 4 3 2 1

ISBN 978 1 4062 1312 6 (paperback)
14 13 12 11 10
10 9 8 7 6 5 4 3 2 1

British Library Cataloguing in Publication Data
Royston, Angela.
  Mites and bites. -- (Disgusting body facts)
  1. Mites--Juvenile literature. 2. Bites and stings--
  Juvenile literature.
  I. Title II. Series
  614.4'32-dc22

Acknowledgements
We would like to thank the following for permission to
reproduce photographs:
Bugwood.org p. **29 bottom** (©Joseph Berger); Getty
p. **11** (©NHMPL); istockphoto pp. **17** (©David Pinn), **29
top** (©seraficus); Photolibrary pp. **9** (©Oxford Scientific
(OSF)/Alastair MacEwen), **27** (©Acha Joaquin Gutierrez);
Photo Researchers, Inc. p. **19** (© Dr. Jeremy Burgess);
Shutterstock pp. **15 top** (©Oberon), **23** (©jefras), **28**
(©Audrey Snider-Bell); Visuals Unlimited, Inc. pp. **7** (©Dr.
David Phillips), **12** (©Dr. Gladden Willis), **15 bottom,
25** (©Dr. Dennis Kunkel), **21** (©Rob & Ann Simpson).

Cover photograph of a mosquito reproduced with
permission of Shutterstock (©Vladimir Vitek).

Every effort has been made to contact copyright holders
of material reproduced in this book. Any omissions will be
rectified in subsequent printings if notice is given to the
publishers.

Some words are shown in bold, **like this**. You can find
out what they mean by looking in the glossary.

Disgusting Body Facts

Mites and Bites

Angela Royston

Contents

Uninvited guests

Many insects and other pests want to share your body! For example, head lice want to live in your hair. Threadworms want to live in your **gut**.

Did you know?

Lice, fleas, and mosquitoes like to feed on your blood. In some countries dangerous spiders and snakes may attack you, too!

Head lice

Head lice bite your **scalp** and suck up some of your blood. The bites make your head itchy. Head lice poo makes your head itch too!

scalp

6

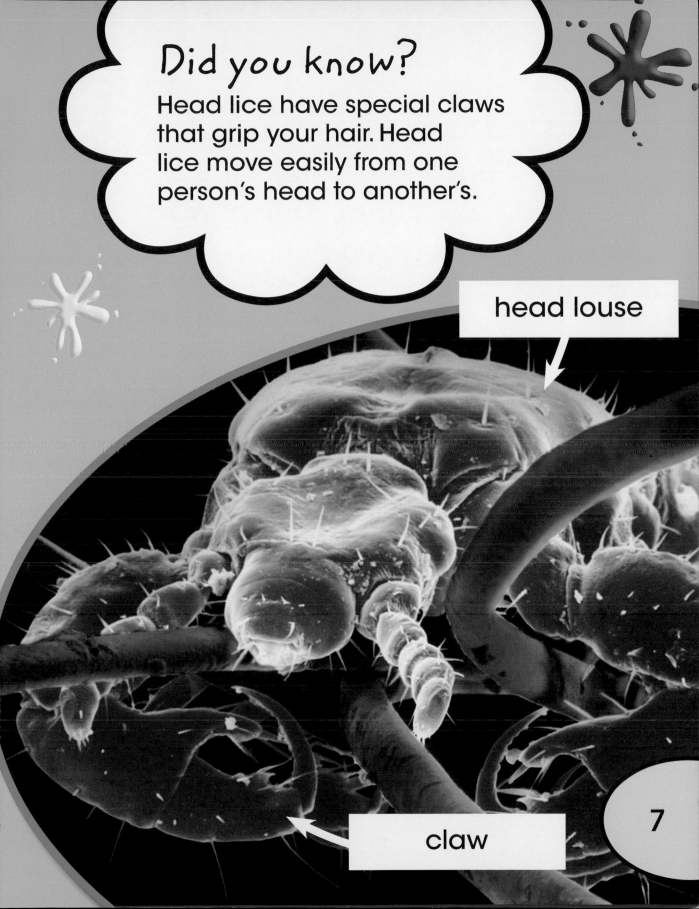

Did you know?

Head lice have special claws that grip your hair. Head lice move easily from one person's head to another's.

head louse

claw

Nits

Head lice lay lots of tiny eggs. They glue the eggs to your hair. The glue is so strong you cannot pull or wash the eggs off. The eggs hatch after about a week.

head lice

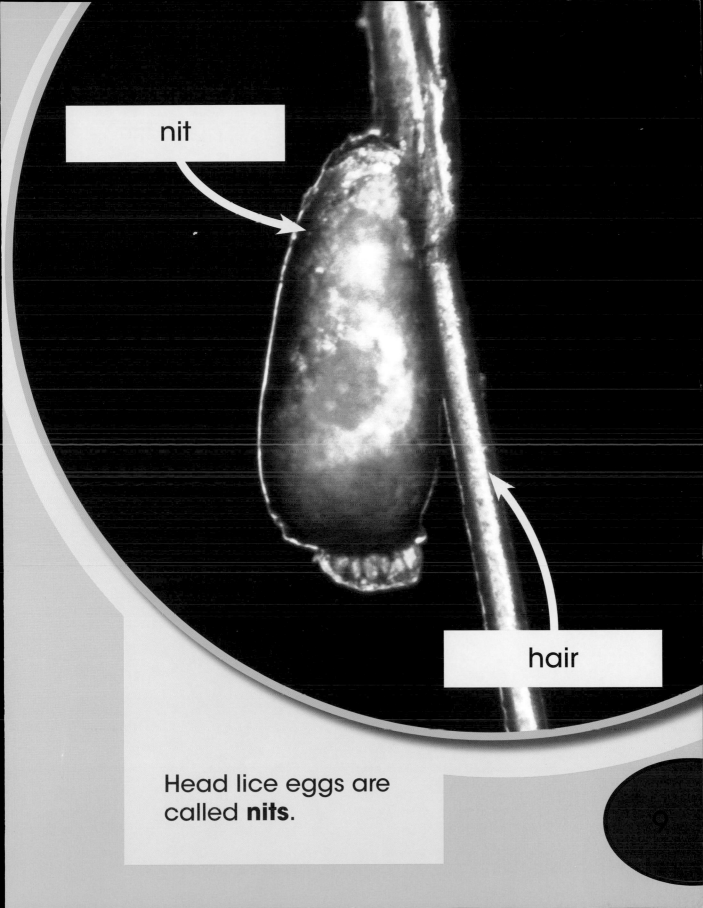

nit

hair

Head lice eggs are called **nits**.

Fleas

Fleas have long back legs. They use them to jump from one person to another. Fleas bite your skin to feed on your blood. The bite swells up. It forms a red, itchy lump.

flea bite

long back legs

Did you know?

Fleas lay eggs that hatch into young fleas. The young fleas eat the adult fleas' poo!

Threadworms

Threadworms are tiny white worms that live inside your **gut**. You might see them in your poo. Threadworms lay their eggs around your bottom. This makes your bottom very itchy.

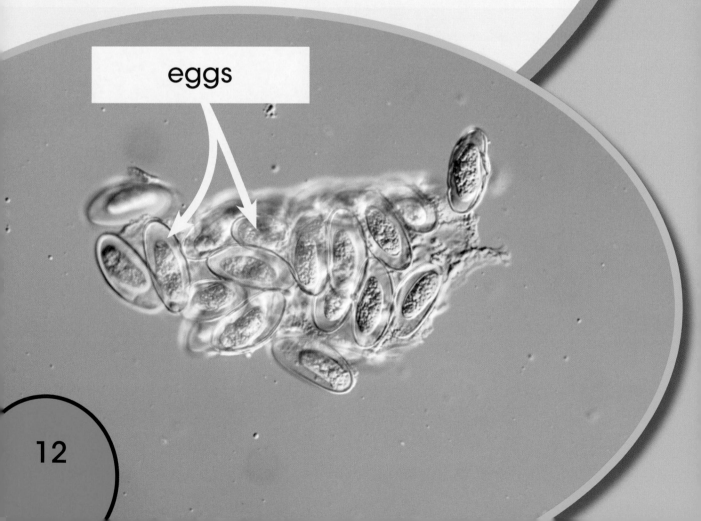

eggs

eggs under
fingernails

Did you know?

When you scratch, some of the eggs get under your nails. When you eat, you swallow some of the eggs. The eggs hatch inside you and new worms crawl out.

13

Dust mites

House dust is mostly tiny bits of dead human skin. Creatures called dust mites live in dust on soft toys and in your bedding. Dust mites are so small you cannot see them!

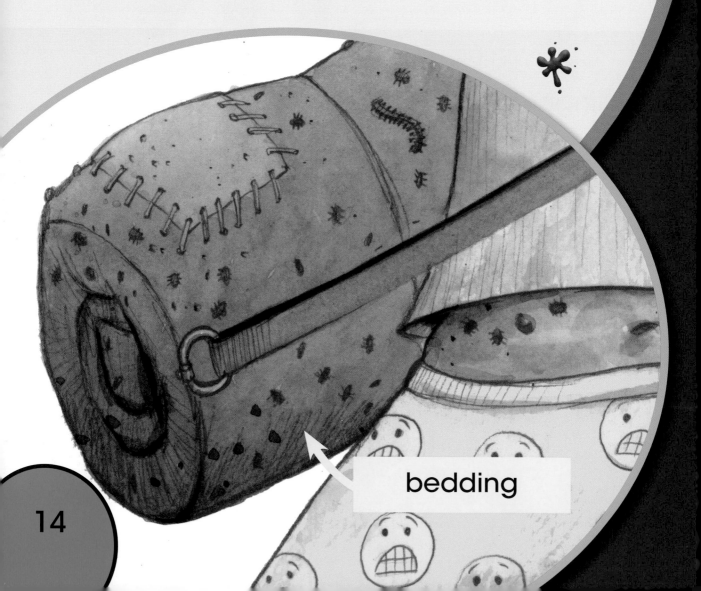

bedding

microscope

dust mites

This is what dust mites look like through a microscope.

Some people are **allergic** to dust mite poo. It gives them hay fever and **asthma,** or trouble with breathing.

Mosquitoes

A mosquito looks for bare skin to land on. Then it bites you. The mosquito sucks up as much blood as it can.

mosquito

Did you know?

A mosquito has a very good sense of smell. It can smell you from **33** metres away. That's about the same distance as **16** beds put end to end!

Bee stings

If a bee stings you, its sting gets stuck in your skin. Bee stings hurt a lot. Things are worse for the bee though. Female honeybees can only sting people once, then they die.

Did you know?

Wasps and hornets do not leave their sting behind. They keep it to use again!

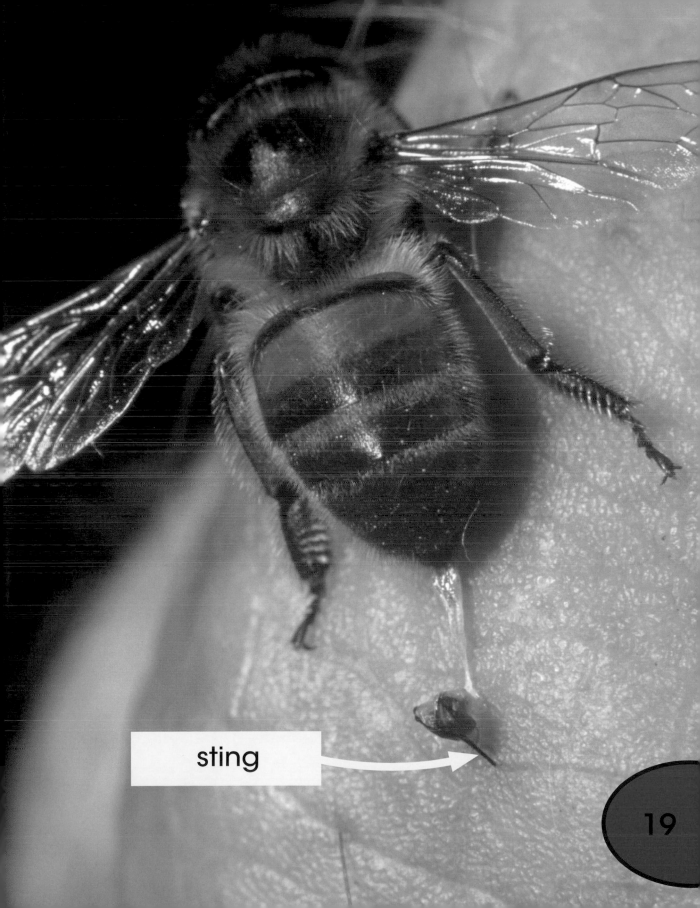

sting

Poisonous spiders

Almost all spiders have poisonous bites. Luckily, only very few can harm humans. These spiders live in warm parts of the world such as Australia and America. Spider bites are painful. They can make you sick and dizzy.

Did you know?

These are some very poisonous spiders:

- Brazilian wandering spider
- American black widow spider
- Australian redback spider
- American brown recluse
- Australian funnel-web spider.

American
black widow

Ticks

Ticks wait on tall grass and trees. Ticks stab your skin with a **probe**, or spike, and suck your blood. You can pull a tick off with tweezers. But make sure you get the whole tick out!

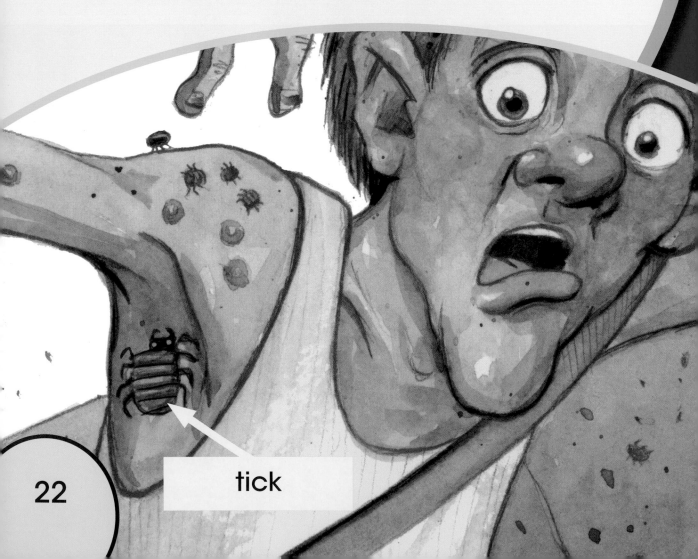

tick

⚠ WARNING

If a tick's head gets stuck in your skin, you must see a doctor. Ticks can give people a dangerous illness called Lyme disease.

Chiggers

A chigger stabs your skin and injects **saliva**, or spit. The saliva mixes with your skin. Then the chigger sucks up the saliva and your skin!

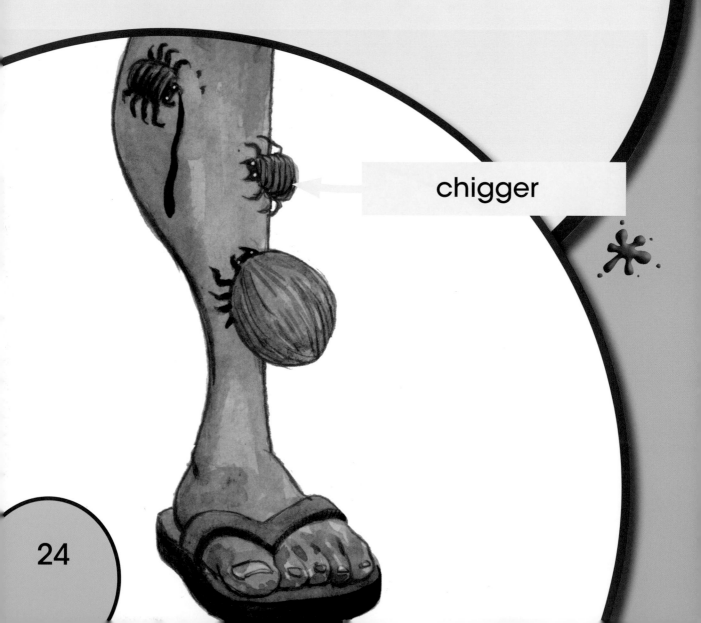

chigger

This magnified photo shows a chigger eating skin.

Did you know?

Some chiggers can be just over 1 mm long. That's about the same size as the full stop at the end of this sentence. Some chiggers are even smaller!

Snake bites

Some snakes have poisonous bites. These snakes have two long fangs. When the snake bites you it puts poison into your blood. The poison is called **venom**. Some venom is deadly.

> **!** **WARNING**
> Venom can make you:
> - sick
> - unable to breathe
> - unable to swallow
> - have a heart attack.

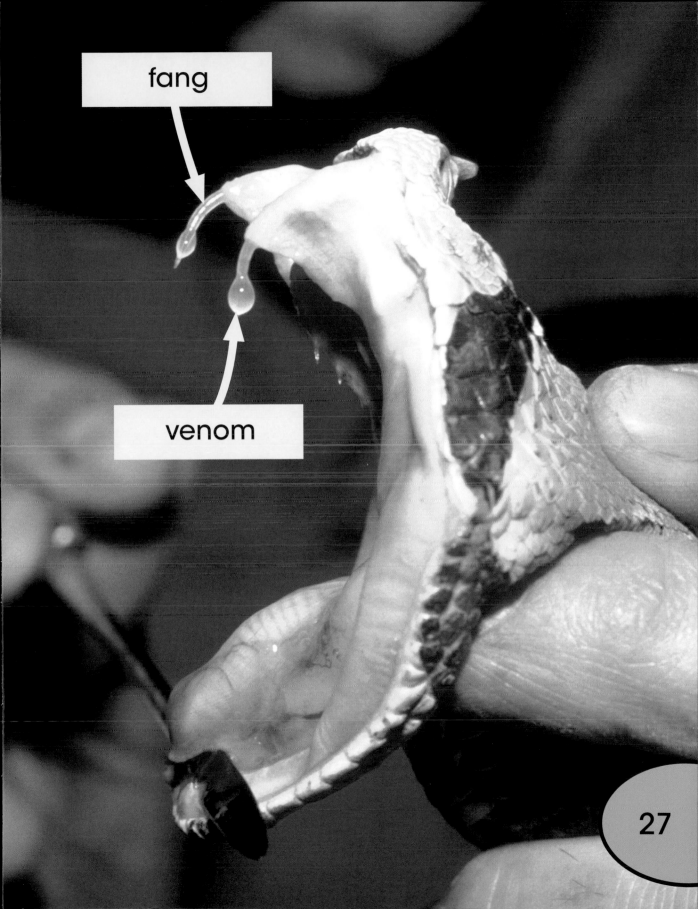

fang

venom

27

More about insects and spiders

tarantula

Some tarantula spiders don't just bite. They can also flick spiky hair into your skin which makes you itch.

A chigger eats your skin for about 4 days. When it has eaten enough, it falls off and changes into an adult.

tick

A tick is a kind of mite. A mite is a tiny member of the spider family.

flea

Fleas are the jumping champions! They can jump up to 200 times their own length.

Head lice start laying their own eggs only ten days after they have hatched.

Glossary

allergic very sensitive to something. When you are allergic to something your body reacts badly to it.

asthma an illness that makes it hard to breathe in and out

gut the long tube that joins your stomach to your bottom

nit the egg of a head louse

probe part of an insect's body which it uses to spike your skin

saliva the liquid made in the mouths of people, insects, and other kinds of animals. Saliva is also called "spit".

scalp the skin on the top and back of your head. Hair grows from your scalp.

venom poisonous liquid made by some animals and insects

Find out more

Find out

Why is the beaver flea famous?

Books

How's Your Health? Nits and Head Lice, Angela Royston (Franklin Watts, 2006)

My Best Book of the Human Body, Barbara Taylor (Kingfisher Books, 2008)

Websites

animals.howstuffworks.com/insects/mosquito3
Use this website to learn about mosquitoes and how they can spread diseases.

kidshealth.org/kid/ill_injure/index.html
Find out about all sorts of different creatures that can bite you on this website.

www.pestworldforkids.org/dust-mites.html
Learn about dust mites on this website. You can also learn more about spiders in the United States through "Pest Games, Pest Detective".

www.nationalfleaweek.com/funFleaFacts.asp
This website has interesting facts about fleas. Click on "Under the microscope" to watch flea videos.

Index